Halifax & Calderdale

by
Ron and Marlene Freethy

Dalesman

THE DALESMAN PUBLISHING COMPANY LTD,
CLAPHAM, via Lancaster, LA2 8EB

First published 1992

© RON & MARLENE FREETHY 1992

ISBN: 1 85568 039 4

Typeset by Lands Services, East Molesey, Surrey
Printed by Peter Fretwell & Sons Ltd., Keighley, West Yorkshire BD21 1PZ

Contents

Cover map by Barbara Yates

INTRODUCTION

ONCE a vital centre of the woollen industry, Halifax is surrounded by old packhorse tracks, turnpike roads, canals and railway tracks pushing along, over and through narrow valleys. This book contains walks along all these routes and also sets out to discover the history and natural history of the fascinating area.

We have always preferred to stroll and explore rather than stride out and walk for the sake of walking and this attitude is reflected in each of the fairly short routes. Our other companion, a black labrador, has also been 'consulted' in the planning of the walks. Wherever relevant we have pointed out picnic sites and suitable pubs serving substantial snacks and well kept beers.

The walks are all-the-year round options, but where there are potential problems with the weather these have been indicated.

Ron and Marlene Freethy

Around Wainstalls
and Cold Edge Dams

*Access: From the centre of Halifax follow the Keighley, Leeds road until you reach Ebeneezer Chapel and the Hangovers Public House. Turn left up Pellon Lane and continue some distance until New Pellon Road is reached. Follow this to the Delvers Inn and fork to the left. Do **not** go left down Wainstalls Lane but follow the bus route through the village. Pass the bus turning circle and follow the narrowing road downhill to a small parking area at Kell Bridge opposite a row of cottages called Bridge Terrace.*

The Route:
AT the bridge find a snicket on the right which is the Calderdale Way Link path. Climb an ancient stone path running above a stream called Kell Brook. At a stone wall turn left and follow the stone path and keeping the old wall on the right. Pass a house with a sturdy wall around it and beyond this bear right across a field towards the Moorcock Inn. Cross the road to the Inn yard and here the route joins the Calderdale Way and passes through a stone stile in the corner. The path follows close to the embankment of a small dam and emerges on to a lane at Moor Bottom. Turn left up the lane for a short distance and turn right over a stile. Cross a field to a footbridge and follow the path uphill keeping a wall on the right until the last field when a stile is crossed and the path twists right and left in a very short distance. Follow the yellow way marker with the wall now on the left. Climb towards Hough Gate Head Farm and follow the signs around this building and across a field to a farm lane and then left to join Cold Edge Road. Turn left along the road and follow this for some distance, but ignore the footpath to the right which is the Calderdale Way. Continue to the Withens Inn and immediately opposite is a farm track. Turn left along this and descend the very rough winding track. Bear right down to Moorlands farmhouse. This stretch can be very, very muddy after rain and treacherous in frost or snow. Follow an obvious track which leads past the derelict Haigh Cote Farmhouse to Haigh Cote Dam and bear right onto the embankment and do not follow the more obvious track down to the left. Eventually descend from the embankment and walk beneath Leadbeater Dam. The two dams together are known as Cold Edge Dams. The path bears left and reaches a rough lane via a stone step stile. Turn right and follow the track to the Moorcock Inn. Ignore the Calderdale Way sign to the right but take the next footpath right which was the route followed on the outward journey.

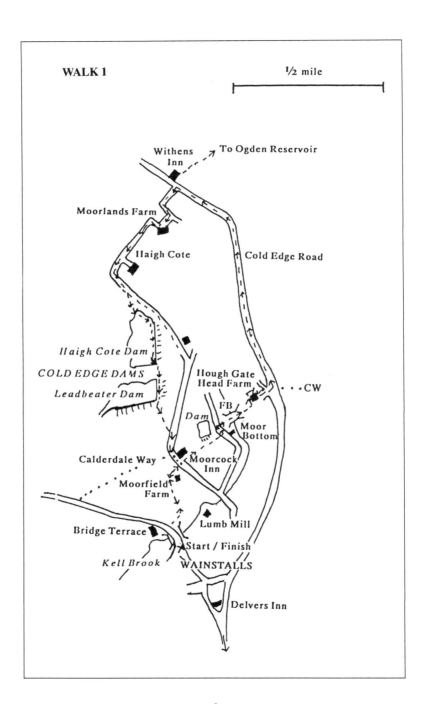

WALK 1

½ mile

Withens Inn
To Ogden Reservoir

Moorlands Farm

Haigh Cote

Cold Edge Road

Haigh Cote Dam

COLD EDGE DAMS

Leadbeater Dam

Hough Gate
Head Farm

···CW

FB

Dam

Moor
Bottom

Calderdale Way

Moorcock
Inn

Moorfield
Farm

Bridge Terrace

Lumb Mill

Start / Finish

Kell Brook

WAINSTALLS

Delvers Inn

Follow this back to Wainstalls and the car. For those with easily controlled dogs this is an ideal walk.

WARNING
This walk is spoiled if attempted in anything but clear weather because its main attractions are the glorious views over moorland and reservoir. It is also not an easy walk if there has been heavy rain, frost or snow. Walkers are, therefore, best advised to choose a pleasant day in the warmer months of the year. Birdwatchers, however, should choose a crisp winter day and on one December walk we watched red grouse and a short-eared owl hunting over the moors by the Cold Edge Dams and even found a couple of its disgorged pellets. Owls swallow their prey whole, digest the flesh and disgorge indigestible fur, feathers and bones through the mouth. These lumps are called pellets and on dissecting the two picked up on this walk we identified the remains of three short tailed field voles and one long tailed field mouse both species being common in the area.

Our Walk:
WAINSTALLS is a compact village set in a pleasant valley and its origins were firstly farming and in the 17th, 18th and 19th centuries its fortunes were firmly based upon the processing of wool. The early stages of this walk prove the connection with woollen mills which were powered by the waters of Kell Brook. At least four mills were so powered. From the bridge where we parked we looked down into the Luddenden Valley and it was easy to see how the mills were totally dependent upon a reliable supply of water and in spells of dry weather the manufacturers must have been very worried indeed. The mills never converted either to steam or electricity and there was thus great incentive to construct reservoirs high on the moor and which form such an attractive section of the walk. Haigh Cote Dam was built as early as 1806 and it was so obviously successful that it led to several mill owners, including some from way down in the Luddenden Valley, joining together to form the Cold Edge Dams Company. This company funded the construction of the Leadbeater Dam, said to have been designed by an engineer of the same name, which came on stream in 1853. The Cold Edge Dam Company has now been absorbed into British Furtex Ltd in Luddendenfoot. Close to their mill is the start of walk No. 7 and they produce upholstery and still need vast amounts of water for washing and dyeing the fabric. Leadbeater is held by the company as a reserve supply but Haigh Cote is now owned by the Halifax Water Ski Company and can be an exciting and colourful place to visit in summer.

The damp field to the left of Kell Brook just past the parking point is lapwing and lark country and both species site their nests among the tussocks of spiky grass. Just by the walls there is a view upstream of what is left of Lumb Mill which already existed in 1803, a small cotton factory later converted to the spinning of worsteds, its machines powered by a huge waterwheel of 36 foot diameter.

Many of our favourite walks involve a stop for a glass of beer or a bar snack and this route affords two opportunities to see how inns evolved. The Moorcock is reached from Moorfield Farm along a track marked by causey stones, almost but not quite covered by grass. The Moorcock was once itself a farm called Moorlands and it still looks more like a farm than an Inn. It is highly likely that during the development of the textile trade the farmer began to supplement his income by selling the surplus of the beer which he brewed for his own consumption and that of his workers. Now selling Websters ales the Moorcock still has a recognisable old barn and outbuildings. Just to the right of the footpath leading from the Moorcock and a sign of the textile age is a small dam built in 1871 to supply water to the steam driven worsted producing Square Mill situated down to the right. There may well have been a cottage industry in these parts before the factory system evolved and even the farmer who owned Moorlands may have done some weaving on the side. The pieces of cloth were dried on tenter-hooks set up in the fields and these were situated near to what is known as the Rope Walk which suggests that yet another local industry thrived in these parts.

We often wonder as we follow this walk if the stretch along Cold Edge Road is worth it, and this is why a good clear day should be chosen as the views on both sides are magnificent. If there is a breeze blowing it certainly lives up to its name and we always remember to wrap up warm whenever we visit Cold Edge Road, but if the walk is planned properly there will be a warm welcome at the Withens Inn, another hostelry which began life as a farm and at almost 1400 feet (426.5 metres) above sea level advertises itself as the highest Inn in West Yorkshire.

From the Withens the track descending to the Dams is our favourite stretch even though it can be treacherous in wet weather. Geese are a feature of the old farmyard and the hull of the boat called the Phalarope is rotting away and well past its sell-by date. Between the farm and the reservoirs we have never failed to find red grouse whatever the weather conditions or the time of the year. We have seen kestrels hovering over the moor and carrying prey back to the nest in the ruins of Haigh Cote Farmhouse which is known to have existed since 1624. Although the water-skiers on the dam do disturb the waterfowl they usually only move off to Leadbeaters and return again to roost in the evening. Whilst the bird species seen is not extensive they do add interest to the walk. In the course of four visits our list includes moorhen, coot, mallard, teal, wigeon, goldeneye, goosander and two species of grebe, the great crested and the dabchick.

Although there is a choice of two hotels there are plenty of picnicking areas along the route, especially close to the dams. This walk shows how industry has developed without interfering with the wildlife of the moorlands.

Around Ogden Reservoir
and Moor

Access and Parking: From the A629 Halifax to Keighley road turn at the Causey Foot Inn as indicated by a brown sign to Ogden Water. Near the reservoir wall you will notice a small parking area and toilets down to the left by the dam. Ignore this area but turn sharp right to reach the split level Rock Hollow car park, choosing the upper level. From here there are splendid views over the reservoir and for those without binoculars there is a coin operated telescope. There are also a number of picnic tables.

The Route:
FROM the lower car park reached via stone steps, turn right to the road end and take the second of the two gates. Here you have a choice. The first gate leads on to the path which runs all the way around the reservoir through and alongside a fringe of mixed woodland, but also with good birdwatching over the water. This is ideal for families with children or those who only have time for a short walk. For the really energetic, the reservoir circuit can be done after the main walk. For those intent on a moorland hike take the second gate and keep the plantation on the left. Follow the rough road and at the fork hold hard left along a footpath in preference to the more obvious quarry road. Once you leave the shelter of the plantation you are on open hillside with old quarries to the right and Ogden Clough down to the left. Descend to a wooden footbridge and cross the end of a retaining wall of the stream. This is a popular picnic area with man made cascades of water leading down from the wall. The wall serves to filter out unwanted gravel from entering the reservoir lower down. Climb from the bridge up a steep flight of stone steps on to the peaty moorland and follow a rough, often wet track marked at intervals by piles of stones. This at 1380 feet (420 metres) is the highest point reached on the walk. Soon in view is the white painted Withens Hotel which stands out clearly on the horizon. The path joins a more substantial track and a left turn away from the Withens should be made unless the time is right and you fancy a glass of Taylor's Landlord beer, rightly famous hereabouts, and described in walk No. 1.

Halifax now comes clearly into view on the right of the Ogden Golf Course. Some of the greens are close to the path so those whose dogs enjoy a walk with them should ensure their pets are on a lead. Wainhouse Tower is a prominent feature down in Halifax.

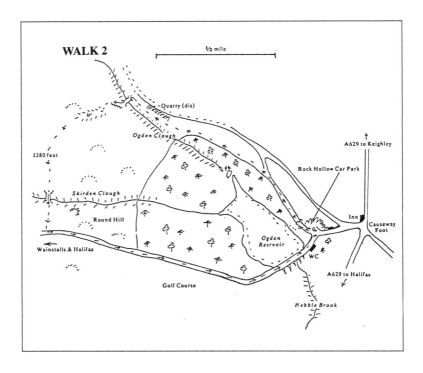

WALK 2

½ mile

Quarry (dis)

Ogden Clough

A629 to Keighley

1380 feet

Rock Hollow Car Park

Skirden Clough

Round Hill

Inn

Causeway Foot

Wainstalls & Halifax

Ogden Reservoir

WC

A629 to Halifax

Golf Course

Hebble Brook

The very obvious track leads downhill, with a mixed woodland plantation to the left, and eventually reaches the dam with the reservoir on the left and Hebble Brook emerging down to the right. After the toilet block and picnic tables on the right the walk is concluded at the end of a slight incline at the Rock Hollow car park.

Our Walk:
WE have walked this route in all seasons including the autumn of 1991 when there was no water in the reservoir at all. Yorkshire Water were repairing the dam, but it gave us a chance to see wading birds feeding in the mud rather than wildfowl roosting on the water. We watched redshank and dunlin both of which we expected to see and a dozen or so ringed plover which came as rather a surprise. Also feeding in the muddy pools was a mixed flock of wagtails with the pied species for once being outnumbered by the grey which is one of the most attractive of our British species. This was obviously an autumnal migration flock but we have seen both species on each of our many walks on this route spread over each of the seasons.

Ogden Water has long been popular with local people but the

facilities on offer are rapidly improving, thanks to the combined efforts of Yorkshire Water and the Calderdale Leisure Services funded by the Countryside Commission. The area now even has its own warden. Ogden was one of the first reservoirs completed to slake the thirst of the industrially developing Halifax and it came on stream in 1857.

By the car park the botanical scene is dominated by introduced rhododendron which look at their best in early summer plus native gorse, and the plantation overlooking the reservoir is also a mixture of introduced trees including larch and spruce along with native species such as Scots pine, birch, rowan and sycamore. The latter is said by some botanists to have been introduced from the Balkans during the 16th century whilst others insist that, like its close relative the field maple, sycamore is native to Britain. Such a mixed woodland attracts a variety of birds including goldcrest, mistle thrush, woodpigeon and sparrowhawk.

As the steep climb leads up into Ogden Clough the high moor is open to the wind and as we reached the highest point of the walk we spotted a fox gliding smoothly through the heather, his brush twitching in the breeze. Here too is an interesting variety of birds including red grouse, meadow pipit and summer visiting wheatears.

The view backwards towards Queensbury is a delight on a pleasant day, especially in winter, but this is not a route to be attempted in snow, heavy rain or low cloud. On such days it is better to stick to the low level circuit of the reservoir when the bird watching can be exciting.

The descent from the High Withens area provides excellent views of one of the highest and windiest golf courses we know and to play it well you need to be a cross between Nick Faldo and Sherpa Tensing! Beyond and below the golf course Halifax can be seen nestling in a fold of the Pennine Hills, and one of its most prominent features is the Wainhouse Tower.

As we continued our walk we watched goldcrests in the fenced off plantation to the left of the track which despite the wire boundary offers clear views into the trees. Here over the years we have seen green and great spotted woodpecker, fieldfare, redwing, jay and on one exciting day a flock of crossbills feeding on larch cones at the height of a January snowstorm.

There is also good bird watching from the dam wall a few yards downhill especially when the reservoir is full of water. Wintering wildfowl include tufted duck, pochard, goosander, goldeneye and Canada geese with the occasional flock of whooper swans stopping off on winter passage over the Pennines.

From the dam the car park is soon reached and as usual we looked forward to spreading out our lunch on one of the picnic tables overlooking Ogden Water.

Around Sowerby

Access: From Halifax cross the River Calder at Sowerby Bridge and follow the signs for Oldham and Ripponden. Turn almost immediately right to Sowerby. Follow the main road to St Peters church and opposite it is the Church Stile Inn. Between these two is Queen Street where there is plenty of quiet parking.

The Route:
FROM Queen Street approach Church Stile Inn and turn left down Pinfold Lane. At the cottages on the right bear right down a little ginnel, the entry narrowed by metal posts and on to Wood Lane. This descends steeply past Wood Lane Hall. Continue to the bottom of Wood Lane which funnels straight ahead into a very narrow path lined with bramble and a millstone grit wall. Cross the railway bridge – the line is still busy and on the right pass a footbridge over the River Calder. Do not cross the bridge but continue on and beneath the railway and climb stone steps to an obvious track. The path forks left. This route passing through a stile into fields is obvious with a number of well maintained stiles. Pass a farm which specialises in equestrian areas which are sometimes in exciting use. Climb towards cottages and climb another stile out on to a road. Turn left and at Finkle Street cottages turn right and pass the cottages on the left. Pass Swamp Dam and turn left and climb steeply through a tree lined clough and follow the stream to Boulderclough. At the summit of the path turn left. Pass houses and just before a main road, turn right and follow a narrow ginnel to another road. Turn left and cross road turning immediately right up a bridlepath. Pass through gates and this reaches another road at Hamer Stones Farm. Turn left and descend through Sowerby. Pass Star Inn on right and continue to St Peters Church on the right. Queens Street and the car is on the left.

Our Walk:
FIRST time explorers will need encouragement at the start of this walk as they look up at the dark millstone grit walls of the Victorian Church of St Peter and across the road the Church Stile Inn. Have faith and enjoy both the walk and the pub refreshments on offer.

Some care is needed in descending Wood Lane to the Hall which is so steep that it can be treacherous after snow, heavy rain or especially after frost. Wood Lane Hall was built in 1649 – there was not much building went on in England during Cromwell's Commonwealth but this is a fine residence. The route leaves the hall on the right, but a good view of the hall can be had without disturbing the residents, by following a narrow path to the right. If

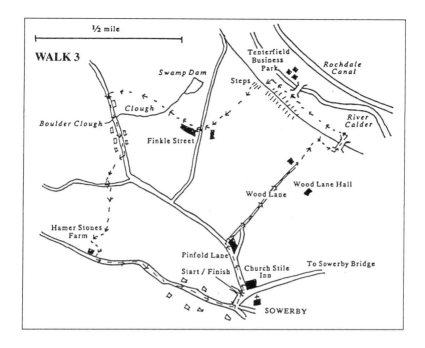

Wood Lane Hall was set anywhere but in an industrial valley it would be on every tourist's list – it really is a gem.

We try to do this particular walk each autumn when the blackberries are at their best. Few lanes are so narrow or so over-hung with bramble which makes collecting blackberries an easy occupation. After our visits to Sowerby and Wood Lane Hall we have stewed blackberry, made blackberry pie, brewed blackberry wine, made blackberry jelly and as we walk we do eat a goodly number of the ripe juicy fruit. Any picker should leave enough for the wildlife and many birds and animals including long tailed field mice, grey squirrels and even the occasional red fox, enjoy a meal of blackberries. Birds on the visiting list include woodpigeon, starling, mistle thrush, jay, blackbird and greenfinch. Close to Wood Lane Hall is a substantial line of poplars which in late autumn make a convenient roost for fieldfares and redwings resting after their long migratory journey from Scandinavia. The natural history is enriched throughout this walk and on the walls leading to the railway bridge and on the bridge itself, we found several species of fern plus groups of wood sage, and crushing the leaves brings back thoughts of Christmas.

Beyond the railway is an extensive area of woodland with the open areas dominated by heather and the woodland areas

13

dominated by splendid young oaks which typically retain their orange-brown leaves throughout the winter. There are also areas of rose-bay willow-herb which in late September have succulent leaves which are fed upon by the larvae of the elephant hawk moth, creatures which are around 10cms (4 inches) and the anterior end does indeed look like the trunk of an elephant and the colour is also similar. Parts of this area can be very wet and if it has been raining, wellingtons are useful and if not wellingtons then good boots are essential.

As we ascended to the farm we watched a herd of contented horses cropping grass with others being rounded up to go through their paces in the well appointed equestrian area which includes an exercise ring and a series of low jumps. Beyond Finkle Street cottages is Swamp Dam which possibly provided a water supply to feed the steam locomotives which had a hard job to do on these steep inclines and used a good deal of water. These days the dam is the haunt of dragonflies and reed buntings. Reed buntings are often overlooked by those beginning the study of birds since they bear more than superficial resemblance to the ubiquitous house sparrows which are never usually given a second glance. Reed buntings are 15cms (6 inches) long with the males having a black head and throat and a very prominent white collar and for those who take care he presents no identification problem. It is the female, however, which causes the confusion with the female house sparrows. A hen reed bunting has a brown head but the buff-coloured eye stripe and throat distinguishes her from the sparrow, as also do the clearly seen moustachial stripe and the white outer portion of the tail.

From the dam we continued to enjoy a day of fascinating birdwatching by climbing through the steeply wooded clough which has breeding treecreepers, blue, great and coal tits, whilst in winter the area provides cover for long tailed tits and flocks of fieldfares and redwings. Long tailed field mice and bank voles are common here and provide food for tawny owl, weasel and stoat. This is cold country in winter and the snow can often come early enough and lie long enough to ensure that the occasional stoat turns white in winter. In this condition they are known as ermines, but they can always be identified as stoats by the fact that the end of their tail remains black. Stoats are larger than weasels and even in their normal brown coat the tip of the tail is always black.

On the final lap of this walk we are always surprised at how quickly Sowerby changes from a small weaving village with cottages typical of the 18th and early 19th century to a modern community area with new houses and a shopping centre which is efficient but just like one thousand and one others. Sowerby, however, does have attractive and unique areas and this walk takes us through this history and areas of lovely countryside which industry has thankfully failed to obliterate.

A Triangle round Sowerby

Access: From Halifax by crossing the River Calder at Sowerby Bridge and turn right towards Sowerby. Almost immediately the main road bears right, we take left fork up Quarry Hill and pass high rise flats and on a bend is St Georges Church typified by its low square tower and dark gritstone church. Continue past church into Haugh End Lane. Beyond are new houses followed by old houses on right. There is ample parking on the left.

WARNING
Some of this walk can be quite wet, so strong shoes or wellingtons are recommended. There are also three very steep areas which those who get short of wind should take very carefully. Towards the end of the walk is an old mill now used by a transport company. The property is guarded by chained rottweilers which sound horrendous but are well secured. We have taken our labrador on this walk and also followed the route several times without him. If you have a dog we suggest that you reverse the recommended direction of the walk as this way you can divert along an obvious section of disused railway line and keep the views of the guard dogs to an absolute minimum.

The Route:
GO to the end of Haugh End Lane. Take track off to the right up Brockwell Lane. At the little settlement of Brockwell there is a potential confusion as it seems to enter private property. Have courage as the official path leads between two round gate posts through the heart of the hamlet of restored houses. It then veers left and around what was Brockwell mill pond but these days it is not easy to see. Pass through a gateway and alongside the top wall of the field. This stretch can be quite muddy until you reach a stone stile. Climb this and turn hard right up a long line of stone steps to Ryburn School. The path turns left in front of the school and then right around the perimeter of its playing fields. It makes sense to time your walk to avoid school breaks or arrival and departure times. At holiday times or weekends the area is of course quiet. From the school pass through a kissing gate and into a field across to a road. Turn left to Field House, a huge house on the right. Immediately opposite is a set of gate posts leading to a carriageway. Turn left along this and descend to a group of houses and eventually one with a walled garden on the left. Opposite this is a very narrow flagged track. Turn right along it and descend to the main A58 road. This can be very busy. Cross it and turn right. This area is called Triangle and continue to Stansfield Mill Lane

which is very obvious. Turn left. Cross a bridge over the River Ryburn. Climb steep hill and pass the site of the old Triangle Railway Station. Approach a railway bridge and find a not very obvious footpath leading into woods. Follow this which has the river down to the left and the old Rishworth railway down to the right. Continue to a complex of mills. Do not turn left over the bridge at the first complex of mills but continue along the woodland path to another railway bridge. Do not cross this but turn left. Continue until the path branches. Follow the least distinct of the two and descend to another complex of mills now used by an engineering firm. Turn left by the side of the mills and cross the river. Climb the road to the main road – the A58 again. Cross the road and turn immediately right up a stone flagged track which climbs very very steeply to meet Haugh End Lane. Turn right to the car.

Our Walk:
THIS is a real walk of contrasts with ancient and modern sections alternating but neither seems to interfere with the other. It also is the perfect combination between urban and country scenery. Immediately we left the modern houses on the right a set of lovely old buildings appear to the right. Down to the left is the River Ryburn a tributary to the Calder with the A58 running parallel and a railway also once ran along the same route, but this has been dismantled since the 1960s. We passed Haugh End House with an attached cottage dated 1528 and bearing a white rose plaque. Here was born in 1630 John Tillotson who became Archbishop of Canterbury during the reign of Charles II. What a childhood he must have had as he walked along the valley prior to the building of the Turnpike road in the 18th century and when the Ryburn ran unpolluted and full of fish. The area is still rich in wildlife, but in the 17th century it must have been spectacular. Brockwell Lane is self explanatory as Brock meant a badger. The old route ran above the Rydale Valley and wound its way through woods full of springs of clear water and dotted with badger setts. Badgers still haunt the area and very welcome they are.

Few schools are more beautifully sited than Ryburn, a modern secondary school surrounded by splendid sports fields. Whilst it is probably preferable to follow this walk at weekends or during school holidays, there are some compensations when there are pupils in residence. Children being children always enjoy eating out of doors and it is a full time job keeping litter under control. Scraps of food attract numbers of birds including chaffinch, mistle thrush, pied wagtail and the ubiquitous magpie. Grey squirrels are also regular attenders at this free invitation to lunch.

From the modern school the next stop we always make is in front of the magnificent Georgian mansion of Field House the ancestral home of the Stansfield family. Recently the building has been converted into luxury flats and we cannot imagine any such

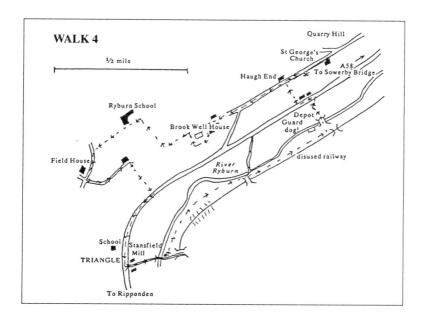

WALK 4

½ mile

Quarry Hill

St George's Church

A58
To Sowerby Bridge

Haugh End

Ryburn School

Brook Well House

Depot
Guard dog!

Field House

disused railway

River Ryburn

School

Stansfield Mill

TRIANGLE

To Ripponden

development with better views. We have heard people complain when large houses are so developed, but surely this is better than allowing them to fall into ruin because one owner cannot afford the upkeep. The notice board outside is labelled Gracious Living Restored – indeed it is.

We then had half a mile of exciting birdwatching with lapwing, skylark, meadow pipit and linnet seen alongside the carriage track leading from Field House across a field and then down past Upper Breck House where the locals obviously feed the birds. Here we listed coal tit, jay, great spotted woodpecker and a sparrowhawk.

Then suddenly we came into the 20th century as we struggled to cross the A58 and then down to Stansfield Mill where the old buildings have been wonderfully restored. The Lodge is an added attraction to the scenery and looked clear as did the Ryburn and as we looked over the bridge we watched a pair of displaying and very noisy dippers and a patient looking heron. Its fishing was soon successful and we watched it wrestle with a reluctant and writhing eel. Those who have the energy for a diversion should explore the now disused railway line reached just after the abandoned site of the Triangle Railway station which was on the old Rishworth branch line. It opened in 1887 and ceased to operate in 1958 although it was used to store rolling stock for a few years afterwards. The line has long been lifted, and nature has taken over. What a joy it is with ferns on the bridges, wild flowers on the

17

banks and native trees on the margins.

From the path between the railway and the river we looked down at the Triangle Cricket Field a really well appointed ground, and the sound of leather on willow adds a pleasant overtone to the song of summer birds. All who enjoy country walking should not be fooled into thinking that this area is too industrialised. In the space of half a mile we felt that we could have been in the middle of a Lake District wood and identified the song of wood warbler, spotted flycatcher, treecreeper and redstart. On a cold winter's morning our labrador disturbed a fox, which jumped down onto the railway track carrying a dead woodpigeon in its jaws. Alongside the old track is a pipe carrying natural gas and the fox used this hump as a launching pad.

Beyond the woodland we eventually reached another point of contrast, but still the birdwatching did not stop. On reaching a complex of old mills by the river we watched a family of grey wagtails and then at the second complex of mill buildings we had a shock and a super sighting. The engineering company have had their share of vandals with their vulnerable yellow painted plant and vehicles being especially at risk. This accounts for the presence of a huge fierce looking rottweiler which roams about at the end of a long rope which looks as if it could hold back the QE2! One thing is certain – only someone with a death wish would enter the yard of the mill. This is why when our labrador is with us we divert slightly and use the railway line as cover just in case. Over the mill we watched a kestrel carrying a rodent in its talons before entering a hole beneath the leaves where its hungry young were waiting to be fed and we could hear their high pitched demands even over the deep barking of the rottweiler.

We always find the final stretch of this walk between the A58 and Haugh End Lane a struggle, the cobbled track being very steep and a great deal of care is needed in wet or icy weather. In the warmer months, however, there is plenty of chances to sit down, enjoy a late picnic and listen to the skylarks which on a good day can drown the sound of traffic – yet another point of contrast in this wonderfully varied walk.

Around Stoodley

Access: From the A646 Hebden Bridge to Todmorden road find a left turn signed Mankinholes and Lumbutts. Cross the River Calder and the Rochdale Canal. Turn right and follow a winding bend and then climb steeply. Towards the top of the hill bear very sharply right still signed Mankinholes and Lumbutts. At Mankinholes just beyond the YHA is a narrow lane to the left of a bend in the road down to Lumbutts. This is visible down in the valley to the right and Stoodley Pike is prominent on the hill to the left.

The Route:
CONTINUE up the lane on which you are parked, which is signed as leading to the Calderdale Way. Cross a stile next to a gate. Over the stile is an ancient causeway leading up from Lumbutts where some walkers prefer to begin their walk. (There is limited parking there opposite the Methodist Church and from which a green fingerpost indicates that Stoodley Pike is 1½ miles and the Pennine Way is ¾ mile).

From the stile turn left up the steep causeway which leads to the junction of the Calderdale and Pennine Ways. From this junction any one of several footpaths can be followed to the Pike across the moorland. From the Pike look downhill over the Calder Valley and see an obvious gate and a stile. Follow the direct path to this but do not deviate along a prominent looking track leading left. This peters out into a very unpleasant boggy area. Do not cross the stile but turn left along another ancient trackway known as London Road which is in fact an old route of 3½ miles from Mankinholes to Hebden Bridge and no doubt beyond this to Halifax and who knows – London? London Road is still a bridleway, and in places it can be very muddy. In wet weather those who can walk without discomfort in wellington boots would be advised to do so. The route passes several farm buildings behind a wall to the right before the circuit is completed at Mankinholes.

Our Walk:
WE choose to begin this walk at Mankinholes because we like Lumbutts! If this sounds strange it is because the view down to this former mill village is magnificent from the car parking area at Mankinholes. Lumbutts is dominated by a peculiar chimney-like structure with a dam above it, now a pleasant little spot popular with water birds. The tower is not in fact a chimney but a housing for three overshot waterwheels, one on top of another, and fed by

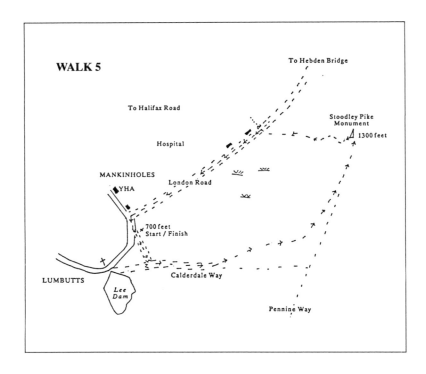

WALK 5

To Hebden Bridge

To Halifax Road

Stoodley Pike Monument

Hospital

1300 feet

MANKINHOLES

London Road

YHA

700 feet
Start / Finish

LUMBUTTS

Calderdale Way

Lee Dam

Pennine Way

a complicated system of dams or syphons. So far as we know this is a unique structure. Fortunately it is now safe from destruction because of the establishment of the Lumbutts Activity Centre based upon the old mill buildings. On offer here are walking holidays, climbing tuition and expert instruction on local history and natural history. There is a comfortable hostel and also self-catering accommodation. This enterprise came into operation in 1991.

There are two other fascinating pieces of history to be seen on this walk – the very obvious Stoodley Pike which dominates the skyline and the often underrated packhorse causeway of stone which is even more of an ancient monument even though we tread upon it! The causeway is particularly obvious between Lumbutts and its junction high on the hill with the Pennine Way. In the days of the packhorse these indeed were the High Roads. In the valley below, the problems of drainage were only solved in the late 18th century when Turnpike roads were laid and the Rochdale Canal was cut. Turnpikes came late to the Pennines because they were expensive to build in hilly undulating districts and therefore the packhorse tracks lasted longer. This stretch is acknowledged as one of the finest of those remaining and was no doubt used by those engaged in the building of Stoodley Pike.

There is often an argument concerning the reason for the construction of the tower. The Pike was erected to celebrate the surrender of Paris and Napoleon's abdication and exile to Elba in 1814. Before the monument was completed, however, "Old Boney" escaped and made one final and fatal bid for glory at Waterloo. This time he was sent to St Helena from which there was no escape.

At a height of 120 feet (37 metres) the Pike is set at the top of a 1310 foot (399 metres) hill and the view from the observation platform is truly panoramic. Following storm damage the monument was extensively restored in 1856.

The Pike is an ideal place for a sheltered picnic and perhaps a spot of birdwatching at the same time. Such areas are bound to be breezy and therefore an ideal habitat for the kestrel which earns its name of the "windhover" and we have seen it using the Pike as its own lookout post. Lapwing and golden plover are also a feature of the area which is at its vibrant best in spring when skylark and meadow pipit are both in full song.

There is speculation rather than hard evidence of human occupation around the site of the present Pike once better known as Langfield Moor. Stone Age flints have been found on the hill, and it is said that the bones of an ancient British chieftain were dug up when the foundations of Stoodley Pike were being made. There is much more solid evidence to support the presence of a beacon fire here from the time of the Spanish Armada of 1588 to the end of the Napoleonic Wars. Here was part of a chain including Pendle Hill above Clitheroe and Beacon Hill above Halifax.

The descent from the Pike should be taken slowly in order to enjoy the view and appreciate how industry slowly crept down from the hills into the Calder Valley. Gone, or almost gone are the old handloom weavers dwellings and farms linked by packhorse causeways. These have been replaced first by water-powered and then by steam-driven mills which were so efficient that they required ever faster and more efficient transport systems. Clearly visible is the ribbon of the Rochdale Canal a 33 mile cut through the Pennines between Manchester and Sowerby Bridge and requiring no fewer than 92 locks to lift the boats up over and down the hills. Also running along the valley bottom is a railway track and the A646 built by a Turnpike Trust in the late 18th century.

Our route, however, stays on the ancient highroad called London Road and as we followed this back to Mankinholes we watched a lapwing incubating her eggs and a couple of brown hares chasing each other in ascending spirals up and over the slopes below Stoodley Pike – a fitting end to a walk brimful of history and natural history.

Around Shibden

Access and Parking: Depending upon how energetic you feel, you may wish to park above or at Shibden Hall rather than in the lower car park by the boating lake. Shibden Hall itself is signed from Halifax town centre off the A58 to Leeds. Entrance to the lower park is from Gofley Hill close to the junction of the A58 with the A6036 to Bradford. The entrance gates are on the Halifax side of the Stump Cross inn and the route descends steeply to the car park and toilets. Care should be taken as there are several ramps to ensure that cars slow down. There is a footpath connecting Shibden Hall with the boating lake park below.

The Route:
FROM Shibden Hall descend through the parkland to the boating lake and the bottom car park. Explore the hall, or for those who do not feel extra-energetic the walk could be started from the lower car park. Go out of the bottom gate and cross Shibden Brook and climb the steep cobbled road to the main A58. Take great care in crossing over towards the Stump Cross pub. A little care is needed at this point to find the correct route as it is not signed. Ignore the sign which indicates the Calderdale Way. Just beyond the bus stop walk towards Halifax for a short distance to a narrow gap in the wall. This leads down to Piggs Gate which is a cobbled path which descends to a group of allotments and old cottages. On passing the cottages the route becomes obvious as a set of large flat stones set into the fields. These and Piggs Lane can be very slippery so care is needed. The path leads to a stile below Spa house and then climbs to a bridleway. A right turn leads past Hallhouses and down a steep hill to the Shibden Mill Inn. Pass through the large car park and turn left along a metalled road. The old mill dam is on the left and Dam Head House on the right. Follow the brook along Simm Carr Road and cross the Calderdale Way, again resisting the temptation to follow it. Pass Lower Lime House, a pleasant building on the left, after which the road becomes a steeply climbing track. The latter soon narrows and forks right to Addersgate Farm. Pass through the farmyard via two gates at which point the route does follow the Calderdale Way for a short distance. This then joins another metalled road and this is followed for a short distance until it turns sharp right at a large water trough. Continue following the road to the right and passing Blake Hill End and then down Brow Lane. Turn right down a cobbled track known as Whiskers Lane. Eventually the cobbles run out and the narrow track continues downhill. Just before a house called Millstream a stone causeway called "The Dicken"

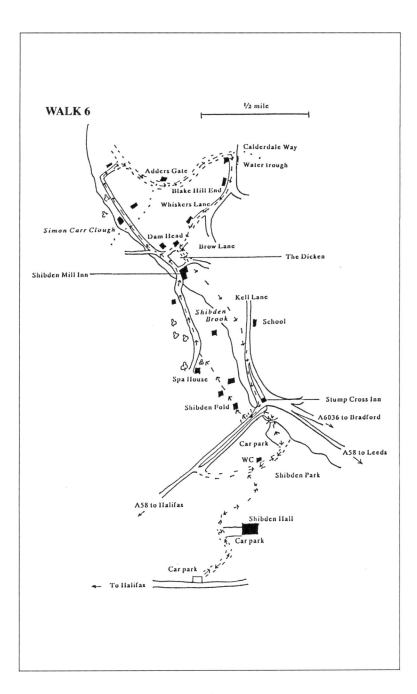

WALK 6

½ mile

Calderdale Way

Water trough

Adders Gate

Blake Hill End

Whiskers Lane

Simon Carr Clough

Dam Head

Brow Lane

The Dicken

Shibden Mill Inn

Kell Lane

Shibden Brook

School

Spa House

Stump Cross Inn

Shibden Fold

A6036 to Bradford

Car park

A58 to Leeds

WC

Shibden Park

A58 to Halifax

Shibden Hall

Car park

Car park

To Halifax

leads off to the left. Follow this across a minor road, through a stile on to a field path, which also has a stone causeway running across it and there are a number of wooden seats. Follow this track as far as Kell Lane and then find the cobbled Staups Lane leading down to the right. This joins the A58 road at Stump Cross and then continues back to Shibden Hall and the car parks.

Our Walk:
DEPENDING upon the weather, a look around Shibden Hall should be enjoyed either before or after this stimulating walk. The attractive house, now a museum is well worth the small entry fee. Shibden Hall has a timber base with stone cladding and the earliest parts date to around 1420. Obviously such an important building has changed over the centuries and it is fitting that it should have period rooms reflecting its history. There is a good collection of 17th and 18th century furniture and outside is a 17th century barn containing a display of horse drawn vehicles.

From the hall there is a lovely stroll down through some 90 acres of rolling parkland which is a mass of bluebells in spring, and in all seasons grey squirrels are likely to descend from the high branches of the trees in order to beg food from picnickers. There is plenty to amuse the children here, before or after their walk, including a narrow gauge steam railway, a tractor train, playground, bouncing castle, pitch and putt and a boating lake. This is not only a walk from your car but also a chance to allow a family to enjoy a day in the countryside.

Shibden is not just a town park but the start of a magnificent country walk which deserves a full day all to itself. It has to be admitted that its start is anything but pleasant but do not despair – keep going! At the top of the steep cobbled road is one of Yorkshire's busiest roads. Once Pigg Gate has been found care needs to be taken during the descent over the cobbles to the allotments and the 17th century cottages especially after heavy rain or a winter frost. Here we watched a flock of long tailed tits moving through a patch of brambles and elderberry. The architectural treasure hereabouts is the Field House built in the 18th century on a site once occupied by the Knights of St. John of Jerusalem who were often rewarded by the Lords of the manors with gifts of land. The rents of these generated cash to support their crusades against the infidels in the Holy Land. From the cottages above the Field House the footpath is obvious as it strikes straight across a field and is inset with huge flat slabs of gritstone and this was a track which saw a few pilgrims of its own during the late 18th and early 19th centuries following the discovery of the value of mineral rich springs in the town of Spa in Belgium. Any mineral rich waters were thereafter called spas and close to a stile is a rusty looking puddle above which is the remnants of Spa House, a popular place in Georgian times and which almost, but not quite, developed into a mini Harrogate.

The rural tranquillity of this walk continues downhill to a stream which is overlooked by Shibden Mill Inn now a very popular hostelry serving substantial bar snacks but it also has a fine restaurant. This is an ideal half way point to have a rest, a meal and we can never resist a glass of Ruddles Ales. For more than 600 years Shibden Mill ground corn using the power of Shibden Brook to drive its huge wheels of millstone grit which dominates the geology of the area. It is good to see how well the area has been restored, although the old mill lodge is now rapidly silting up. It will soon be dominated by trees, especially willow and alder although there are still plenty of water plants such as yellow flag iris and water forget-me-not. We spent some time watching reed buntings and a family of moorhens using what remains of once open water. Dam Head House still stands and has been beautifully restored. Its exterior seems to be 17th century although much of it dates to the 15th. It is, however, privately owned and walkers should always respect other people's space.

We followed Shibden Brook and watched a pair of dippers feeding by submerging to get at the stonefly and mayfly larvae thus proving that the stream is fairly clean. Beyond Addersgate Farm – the occasional adder does live up here – we watched a flock of lapwings down on the fields close to the brook and there was also a pair of curlew and a solitary partridge. On the hillside on the opposite side of the valley is the ruin of Scout Hall built around 1680 but during 1991 restoration work was going on.

Prominent – indeed dominant – up to the left are what are known as Jubb walls which were built to ensure old quarry excavations are prevented from slipping down on to the roads. Our descent of Whiskers Lane presented a twofold problem. Firstly, how did it get its name and secondly how do you keep your feet on the steep slippery slope. We don't know the answer to the first question, but good strong shoes or boots are essential to prevent slipping. This is, however, one of the most attractive parts of the walk, but care is needed not to miss the left turn into The Dicken. If you suddenly find Millstream Cottage on your right you have gone too far and must retrace your steps for a few yards.

By the time the minor road has been crossed the wooden seats set into the contours of the field are welcome especially if you have resisted the temptation to have a bar snack at the Shibden Mill Inn, and have brought your own picnic. From one of these seats we watched a pair of jays chasing each other through the trees, their white rumps flashing in the sunlight. Up high to the left Salterlee School with its attractive little bell tower can be seen. The flagstones along the footpath mark the one time carriageway to Springfield House from Stump Cross. The footpath remains splendidly rural and is one of the least spoiled in all Yorkshire.

Luddendenfoot and Branwell Brontë

Access: Turn left from the A646 Halifax to Hebden Bridge road just before the traffic lights at Luddendenfoot. If you see the Weavers Arms and the Coach and Horses you have gone too far. The best landmark is the British Firtex Mill on the right with the turn opposite this building. Immediately you have turned left and crossed the canal bridge there is another very sharp left turn into a car park sandwiched between the Rochdale Canal and a children's playground. There are no toilet facilities here.

The Route:
FROM the car park go out towards the bridge and turn left. Cross the bridge over the River Calder into Station Road. At its junction with Old Station Road bear left up a very steep cobbled road with a hand rail on the right hand side. This emerges on to Belle View Terrace. Turn right and continue beyond rows of cottages to the left and right. Beyond these look for a gate stile on the right. This leads to the steep field path which descends to a gate stile into a wood. Cross a stream which can be a problem in wet weather. The footbridge marked on the O.S. map no longer exists but the stream is usually narrow enough to enable walkers to cross using a number of well placed flat stones. At the end of the wood, cross a field to what at first appears a grass track but a close examination reveals causeway stones beneath the surface. The track is narrow and bounded on either side by a solid stone wall. Pass through a group of old farm buildings and then under a railway bridge. The road then bears left and passes on the left of the factory of FKI Tully who make parking meters. Turn right at the end of a group of cottages and cross the bridge over the River Calder. Look at the weir of the old mill down to the right. Pass Clarence House on the left but take care at this point to look to the right for a narrow entry on to the canal towpath between cottages. If you reach the bridge over the canal you have gone too far. Turn right along the Rochdale Canal. Pass two sets of locks on the left and a bowling green and a plant nursery on the right. The towpath crosses Luddenden Brook and then passes under the road bridge to the car park on the right.

Apart from the steep climb at the beginning this is a flat and easy walk. Those who hate steep hills may prefer to travel in the opposite direction to the route indicated as the climb up from the canal to Belle View Terrace is much more gentle. We feel, however, that the views are better from the route we have followed.

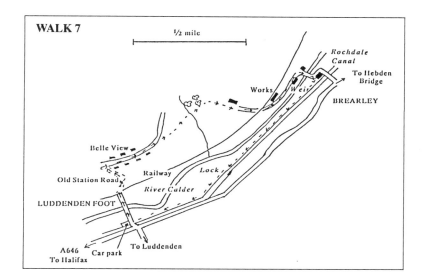

WALK 7

½ mile

Rochdale Canal
To Hebden Bridge
BREARLEY
Works
Weir
Belle View
Railway
Lock
Old Station Road
River Calder
LUDDENDEN FOOT
A646
To Halifax
Car park
To Luddenden

Our Walk:

AS Station Road gives way to Old Station Road we looked in vain for the station long since closed although trains regularly thunder past between Halifax, Hebden Bridge and Todmorden. The old station became famous, perhaps infamous would be a better word, thanks to Branwell Brontë (1817-1848). The unfortunate young man, brother of a bevy of sisters of genius, was far too fond of drugs and alcohol, which dulled his wits and destroyed his undoubted talents as a writer and a portrait painter. At Luddendenfoot he even failed as an assistant ticket clerk and was sacked for "gross misconduct" in 1842. The site of the station is now a developing industrial estate. Those who would like to see what a station was like at this time should visit Hebden Bridge where there is much evidence remaining of the 19th century buildings and even the wooden signs survive intact.

Many walkers, climbing the steep cobbles from the valley wonder why the houses should be so high up away from road, canal and rail links. The reason is that at one time the valley bottoms were insect infested swamps which were frequently inundated as the River Calder flooded. Malaria was not eradicated in Britain until the mid 19th century. Folk therefore lived and worked on the hillsides and the settlements were connected by the packhorse tracks described in detail in Walk No. 5. Such tracks are also a feature of this walk, but they require a more careful look to find them, but what fun we had looking and poking our walking sticks into grass in search of more causey stones. This really is walking through or rather over history.

Once the cottages of Belle View have been left behind, the beautiful views really do begin and as we walked across the green fields we watched horses and cows grazing contentedly between the high path and the valley. Traffic can be seen moving along the A646 and trains regularly shoot across your vision but they are not at all intrusive especially when you realise that they are very much a part of the history of the area. In any case the noise is muffled by bird song. We watched a treecreeper spiralling its way up the trunk of an oak whilst a great spotted woodpecker was drumming on the hollow trunk of a dead birch. Given a reasonable day there are plenty of sheltered dells on this walk which are ideal for a picnic and we have found the woodland area to be warm even in a January sleet storm.

Whilst passing along the narrow causeway we always keep our eyes on the gritstone walls which are the home for stoats which seem to be residents here. They feed on rabbits, long tailed field mice and short tailed field voles all of which are common in the area. Growing close to the wall are a number of sapling oak trees which in time will provide a wonderful habitat for an assortment of wildlife.

Once on the bank of the Rochdale Canal the wildlife obviously changes but stoats are still resident here. This is, however, pied wagtail, mallard and moorhen country. It is good to see this canal corridor gradually being brought back to life and the two sets of locks are in good repair, although too seldom used. As tourism develops we are sure that this will change. The second set of locks have been dedicated to the life's work of Edward Kilner, a local solicitor.

With the profusion of canalside vegetation and shallow water this is real dragonfly country. They belong to a group of insects called the Odonata which is divided into two groups, the large hawker dragonflies and the smaller and much more delicate damselflies. Both types feed on insects which they catch in a basket-like structure made by clasping together the front pair of their three pairs of legs. Females lay their eggs in water, the sexes mating during a flight when they are attached together in tandem. The larvae are also fearless predators and they develop in the water emerging anything up to four years later depending upon the species. On emerging from the aquatic pupae the adults dry their wings in the sun whilst hanging on to waterside plants before their brief period of adult life. They are just as predatory as their larvae and are just as territorial as birds. On this stretch of canal the large brown aeshna dragonfly is very common, but is outnumbered by the delicate and delightfully attractive blue damselfly.

What a pity that Branwell Brontë, such a potentially brilliant artist and writer did not spend more time walking along the canal and less in the numerous ale houses, some of which now provide excellent bar snacks for the tired walker.

Hardcastle Crags and Blake Dean

Access: From Hebden Bridge follow the A646 through traffic lights towards Todmorden. Just beyond a garage use the turning circle to return to the same set of lights. Turn left up the steep hill signed Heptonstall and Burnley. Ignore the Heptonstall signs and continue to a junction signed Colne. Bear right here and pass a one time chapel now a hostel on the left. Continue along the narrow road and keep an eye open to the right for a car park at Clough Hole. The car park is provided by the National Trust who own the woodlands in the valley below. Parking is free although there is a collection box under the information board and contributions are welcome. There are a few picnic tables here.

The Route:
FROM Clough Hole car park descend a steep and winding path to Gibsons Mill. Do stick to the wide main path even though there seem to be shorter but muddier routes to the left. Most of these are blind ended and you finish up having to rejoin the main path after an undignified scramble. At Gibsons Mill cross the Toll Bridge and go around the mill to the left and climb past the old lodge to the top of the estate. At this time you are following part of one of three official nature trails, this one marked by green branded posts. Pass the eroded rocks from which Hardcastle Crags takes its name. The trail then approaches a wooden footbridge and those who only want a short walk should cross this and return to Gibsons Mill.

There is, however, a splendid alternative which returns to the footbridge after an exhilarating diversion. From the bridge which should not be crossed, follow an obvious track which climbs gently and with the wooded valley and bubbling Hebden Water down to the left. At the top of the track pass a cottage on the right and descend through a dell with lots of bracken growing around blocks of eroded millstone grit. Follow the track upwards and through a hole in the wall and into a plantation and then into an area of bracken and old quarry and then up to yet another stile. Down to the left is the remains of an old railway bridge which was part of a single track line built to service the construction of the reservoir at Blakedown at the turn of the century.

There are plenty of sheltered dells on this moorland stretch of the walk which leads to Blake Dean marked by a small belt of trees and the meeting of two little streams. On the opposite side of the main stream is the Hebden Bridge to Colne road. After a rest retrace your steps through the crags. If you feel energetic descend

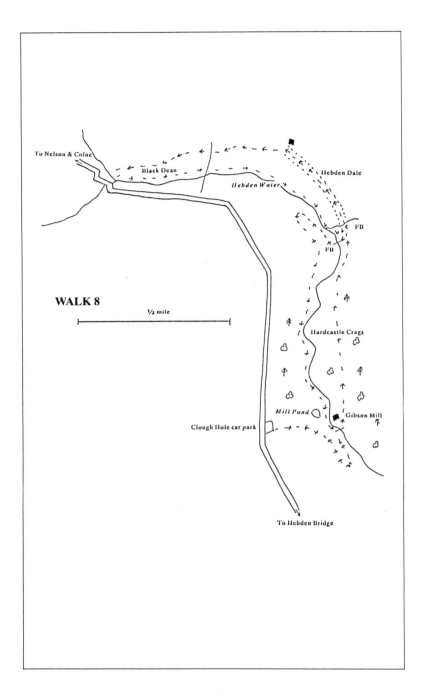

WALK 8

½ mile

To Nelson & Colne
Black Dean
Hebden Water
Hebden Dale
FB
FB
Hardcastle Crags
Mill Pond
Gibson Mill
Clough Hole car park
To Hebden Bridge

from the upper path down one of several wet and narrow tracks to Hebden Water and then turn left. Follow or rather scramble along the not very well defined path which follows the stream through areas dominated by Scots pine to the wooden footbridge. Once more follow the green ringed posts of the nature trail back to Gibsons Bridge passing one mill lodge on the right and another on the left. From Gibsons Mill follow the wide meandering track back up to Clough Hall car park.

Our Walk:

WITHIN two minutes of leaving the car park we had one pleasant surprise which we had hoped for and one which we did not expect and which was not so pleasant. The first was a red squirrel which was feeding on a larch cone. Hardcastle Crags is one of the few places left in England where the native red squirrel is still common and free from competition with the grey squirrel which was introduced from North America in the 1870s. This is why our second sighting was not very welcome for there, as bold as brass, was a grey squirrel the first we had seen in the crags. Grey squirrels are larger than the red and they have smooth ears whilst the ears of the red have tufts of hairs sticking up from them. We also saw a green woodpecker investigating a potential nesting hole making the third notable observation before we reached Gibsons Mill. This marvellous building is certainly not being used to its full potential these days. What a super field studies centre it would make!

The mill built in 1800 once powered by Hebden Water, but in 1860 converted to steam but still failed to compete with the huge factories down in the developing town of Hebden Bridge so close to the canal and turnpike road. Gibsons Mill closed in 1900 and following a revival period between the two wars when it served as a dance hall and roller skating rink it again failed and is now sadly idle.

The wildlife hereabouts is certainly not idle and on our climb through Hardcastle Crags to the cottage we saw not one green woodpecker but three! They were feeding on the larvae of the wood ant, another species not very common this far north. They make huge dome-shaped nests of pine needles and the woodpeckers were scratching away at these to get at the grubs. The ants, as you would expect, do not like this and react by producing a stream of formic acid which some say kills the lice on the feathers of the birds. We could smell the vinegar-like aroma of the formic acid from a distance of more than 20 yards. We took good care to keep away from the ants because they do not sting but bite through the skin and then squirt in the formic acid. This really hurts!

Blackbirds also nest in the woodland areas but once we reached the open moor it was not blackbirds we were looking for but its close relative the ring ousel. These look very like blackbirds but they have a white crescent around the breast. They site their nests among scree especially if it is covered with heather, gorse or bracken. We have often seen them feeding their young in summer. Ring ousels, or mountain blackbirds as they are sometimes called, arrive here from Africa and southern Europe during April and have usually returned to their winter quarters by the middle of October.

Those who stick to the shorter portion of this walk will find good stout shoes perfectly adequate, but those on the longer trek will find it quite muddy in a few areas and there are also stretches of high bracken which can hold a lot of water after rain.

Whatever the weather, Hardcastle Crags will provide plenty of shelter and looks beautiful during a light snow shower but the moorland extension is very exposed and you need to dress accordingly.

Close by the wooden footbridge is a wooden shelter and this can be a cosy spot in poor weather. At the Information Centre in Hebden Bridge it is possible to purchase leaflets about the area and from the town there is a marked walk up to the crags. There is also a car park just off the Hebden Bridge to Keighley road from which a circular walk leads to Gibsons Mill along the banks of Hebden Water returning via a high path through mixed woodland. There is a car parking fee here and there are toilets nearby. Those with a whole day to spare and plenty of energy may be able to enjoy both walks but we guarantee that they would be tired by the end of the day.

Around the Clog Museum, Mytholmroyd and Hebden Bridge

Access: From Halifax follow the A646 towards Hebden Bridge. Walkleys Clog Museum is on the left. This walk can be combined with a visit to one of Yorkshire's most interesting museum complexes, which has good parking. An alternative is to park near Hebden Bridge railway station and vary the starting point slightly. As the walk is clearly circular this presents no problem.

The Route:
FROM Walkley's cross the busy road on to the Canal towpath and turn right. Follow the Rochdale Canal to Mytholmroyd. At the third bridge (only built in 1988) look out for Banksfield and Zion Terrace. Find steps to the right. Ascend these and turn right into the busy centre of Mytholmroyd. Pass beneath the railway bridge and continue to the "Shoulder of Mutton". Bear right and find Elphanborough Close on the right. At the old fire station, still having its red doors, but now a pottery, turn right up Stocks Lane. Find Nest Lane and turn left. Follow the road round to the right and then find a house called Rose Mount. Here turn left up a wide path. There is a signpost here which reads Daisy Bank and Erringden Moor. There is now a very steep climb along a track which is part grass and part stone. Approach stiles leading off to the left and right. Ignore these but continue straight on and climb towards a plantation up and to the right. Cross another well maintained stile and ignore a right turn. Continue past the plantation with a wire fence on the right. There are holly trees on the left and conifers on the right. The steep climb can be muddy in wet weather and slippery in ice. Approach a field gate but do not go through it. Bear to the right and follow the line of the stone wall above the plantation. There are some faded markers to the narrow Old Wall Lane. After passing beneath power lines do not continue straight ahead. This leads to Stoodley Pike (see walk 5) but turn right onto another cobbled lane. Continue to a junction of two more ancient tracks. Do not go into a field but turn left and then almost immediately right into yet another lane. Pass an old house on the right and then a farm also on the right and a house on the left. The lane now descends to Great Jumps and pushes through the buildings and then turns right. Find a stone stile and climb this to follow the bottom edge of the field to another stile. Turn right and head for a line of trees. Cross a stile in the corner of the field and continue to Old Chamber. Cross a lane and find another stile. This leads into a field and in just over 50 yards find a stile to the

left and set into a wall. Cross this. The path crosses four fields and descends through a well marked series of stiles. This leads to Crow Nest Wood. Bear right along a steeply descending path through rich woodland. At the end of this turn right and resist all temptations to turn left. Keep the wall on the left and view Hebden Bridge down to the left. Continue past new houses on the left. Turn left at a T junction. Descend to and pass under a railway bridge, cross a bridge over the river Calder. Hebden Bridge railway station is on the left. Bear left and meet the canal towpath. Cross on to the towpath and turn right. This returns to Walkley's.

Our Walk:
WE love walks with a touch of history and this trek should begin with a visit to Walkley's Clog Mill. Following a disastrous fire the mill reopened in 1991 and the owners took advantage of rebuilding to improve the exhibits. Much of the machinery was metallic and survived the blaze. The displays are impressive, the shop just the place to buy souvenirs and presents and the cafe just the place to have a warm drink before starting the walk. It is, however, the clog making techniques which are the most important feature. Wood from the alder was used to make the clog bottoms and during the walk the trees still grow in many areas. Its scientific name is *Alnus glutinosa*, the latter word meaning sticky, and the young leaves are certainly sticky. Alder produces flowers of two kinds. The male catkins are long drooping structures which appear in autumn and last all winter. They grow in clusters of between three and five and they are dull purple at first and yellow with pollen when ripe. The female catkins are oval and look like small fir cones. They are produced in spring and after being fertilised they ripen. The thick scales of which they are composed separate and allow the seeds to fall out without themselves being detached from the tree. Many seeds fall into water and as they float they allow alder to be spread. The wood is soft and light. If exposed alternately to wet and dry conditions it soon rots, but if kept entirely submerged or buried in damp soil no wood is more durable. It is ideal for the foundations of bridges, water pipes, barrels and for paper pulp. When an alder tree is struck with an axe it oozes sap which almost immediately turns blood red. The Celts believed that the blood came from an evil spirit living within and would not cut the trees down. The old name for the tree was aller and accounts for place names such as Ellerbeck in Yorkshire, Aller in Derbyshire and Aldridge in Staffordshire.

In modern scientific circles the alder has been studied as its roots are covered in small nodules. These are full of bacteria which are able to convert atmospheric nitrogen directly into nitrates and then into protein. Clover and all the pea family have this ability and it means that they are able to grow in soils which are so poor in minerals that most plants are unable to find enough nutrients to survive.

No-one should attempt this route without taking a pair of bin-

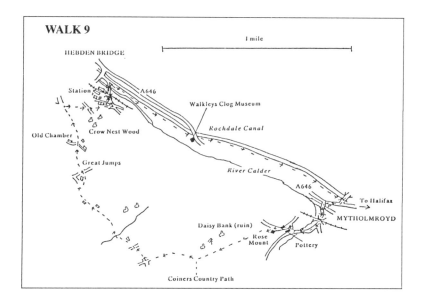

WALK 9

1 mile

HEBDEN BRIDGE

Station
A646
Walkleys Clog Museum

Crow Nest Wood
Rochdale Canal

Old Chamber

Great Jumps
River Calder

A646

To Halifax

MYTHOLMROYD

Daisy Bank (ruin)
Rose Mount
Pottery

Coiners Country Path

oculars. There is always something to see along the canal stretch but it is up on Daisy Bank that the extra magnification is so useful. There are views over into the so called Coiners' country, a quiet spot where David Hartley the King of the Coiners and his gang operated in secrecy. David is buried at Heptonstall and his story is told in walk No. 12. The birdlife up on the heights is interesting rather than numerous and species to look out for are golden plover, redshank, dunlin, curlew and the twite. The latter is an interesting species known as the mountain linnet. It is thought to have had its origins in the highlands of Tibet and spread into Europe during the Ice Age. As the highlands of Britain have become warmer the twite's range has diminished until just a few areas of Scotland, the Pennines and Wales provide a habitat cool enough for it. The twite also shows an unusual form of territorial behaviour, since the male is not interested in a fixed geographical territory but prefers to defend the area around his chosen female. This is a sensible arrangement as it allows the female the space to feed without being molested by eager males. The nests are very often built in loose colonies among heather, but they will use gorse bushes less than six feet (two metres) high. Twites are often not noticed because of their rather nondescript brownish appearance. In winter it can be distinguished by its yellowish bill which changes to a greyish colour in the breeding season. The lores and throat are orange coloured and the male has a rosy pink rump. It is well worth spending time on the upland sections of this walk because the twite is such a rare and interesting species.

Although this walk is around five miles we treat it as if it was ten and take a whole day over it and have a good long picnic in Crow Nest Wood. There is nothing particularly rare in this area but on a hot June day we watched a common lizard sitting on a log sunning itself in the afternoon sun and it is also a good place to watch common butterflies such as small tortoiseshell, green veined white, meadow brown and large heath.

The temptation to pass Hebden Bridge station should be resisted as it is a museum in its own right. The original Victorian wooden signs are still in position and the design is typical of a mid 19th century station and it should be preserved in this condition. For those who don't feel too tired after the walk there is plenty to see in Hebden Bridge and we even know one energetic friend who walked up to Heptonstall before returning to the Clog Mill. This Heptonstall route is our walk No. 11. In Hebden Bridge itself is a good Information Centre and several good inns and restaurants. From the pleasantly restored marina, a horse drawn barge travels along the Rochdale Canal and stops at Walkley's Clog Mill. It passes through a short tunnel and the crew propel the barge through by pushing their feet against the roof of the tunnel. This is called "legging" and the horse is separated from the barge and walked over the road to await the arrival of the leggers.

The attraction of this walk is its variety and whatever your reason for walking, this round trip is bound to provide something of interest. Walkley's itself is worth half a day's visit in its own right. Not only does the mill provide a history of clog making but it is also becoming a shopping centre. The mill was built specifically as a clog mill in 1851 and at one time much storage space was needed to season and dry the alder wood used for the clogs. Now that seasoned wood is brought in, the old storage space is used as a shopping centre. On site are picture framers, two silversmiths, a potter, furniture shop, Japanese shop, toyshop, pet shop, a florist and a kitchen shop. There is obviously an excellent clogger's shop and a good restaurant. In April 1992 the Museum of Childhood moved from Hebden Bridge to a new display area in the Clog Mill.

The mill provides a wonderful focus for this walk. Why not buy a pair of stout clogs or perhaps you prefer your old boots?

North Dean Nature Centre

Access: Leave Halifax on the A629 road to Elland. At a complex junction follow the A6026 to Greetland. When this joins the B6112 follow to traffic lights with West Vale Junior and Infants School on left. Turn left on to the B6113 and then immediate right onto the North Dean Nature Centre car park. There are toilets here. Part of this walk can be followed by the disabled in wheelchairs and these people are allowed to park at the centre itself.

The Route:
FROM the car park cross Black Brook Bridge and follow the footpath around a football field and then climb steps from a garden to Clay House which is the base for the North Dean Information Centre and the start of the Calderdale Way, an increasingly popular long distance footpath. It opens daily in the summer and in winter on Saturdays from 1pm to 4pm and Sundays from 11am to 4pm. From the rear of the Centre follow the signs to the nature trail leading to the old railway track through the woodlands. Keep to the main path ignoring a loop leading to the left which has been designed for those in wheelchairs. Continue until another left loop gives no choice. Follow this round and look out for a gap in a stone wall to the right. Squeeze through this gap and turn right. Pass beneath power lines and ascend to meet an upper path. Do not turn back here but bear right. Look down to see the meeting of the valleys of the Hebble and the Calder. Pass gritstone outcroppings up to the left. Away and up to the right is a good view of the Wainhouse tower. The path climbs steadily but there are plenty of seats alongside the path which are ideal for picnics. At the top of the path do not turn round and follow the upper route to the left. Turn right and descend the stepped path which can be treacherous after rain, snow or heavy frost. Cross a tiny wooden bridge over a stream and continue to a junction with a broader path. Turn left and the route climbs gently before descending again. Turn right and keep a stone wall on the left. The path swings right and then climbs steeply. At the top turn left and join wide path continue almost to the end of the track where care has to be taken. The broad path seems to continue but a smaller path runs almost through 180° and leads to another wide path. This leads to the hole stile in the wall which was squeezed through on the outward journey. Pass through this and turn right. Return to the car park via the Visitors' Centre.

Our Walk:
LIKE walk No. 6 which is based around Shibden Hall, this

pleasant stroll begins at a delightful and historic building. It was built in the 17th century for the yeoman family named Clay who lived in West Vale. There has been a settlement in this area at least since the Bronze Age and from Roman times an altar dated AD 208 was found in the area. Only a replica is on display at Clay House, the original having been removed to the Fitzwilliam museum in Cambridge. The house has high gables and mullioned windows and nearby is a converted old barn. The Countryside Centre has a bright exhibition of the social and natural history of Calderdale. There is an informative display of the history of North Dean Wood through which runs a nature trail for which a leaflet can be purchased. There is a small cafe and a book shop.

The early part of the walk follows the line of a railway track, which was constructed by the Lancashire and Yorkshire Railway Company through Holywell Green in 1875. The track through the wood was a branch line and coal sidings. The line closed in the 1950s and there are a few reminders of the days of steam including a number of huge rotting sleepers.

The railway actually sliced through an ancient woodland which was once part of an old hunting area which was also used by local people to graze their pigs which were allowed to feed upon acorns. This practice was known as the law of pannage. They were not allowed to cut down trees but could collect firewood and could pull down any branches they could reach with a crook and cut with a bill hook. Here is the origin of the phrase "by hook or by crook". Workers who were allowed to cut down trees were the charcoal burners who are known to have operated in North Dean Woods. The woodlanders of old used the wildwoods much as we use Do-it-Yourself stores and it is no wonder that they were almost destroyed. Fuel for the salt industry, smelting of ore and the constant demand for charcoal all added their own unique sounds, sights and smells. Bark was stripped for tanning hides, potash produced to make glass and soap and larger trees were selected for buildings, ships and furniture. The woollen industry expanded rapidly from the Middle Ages onwards and there is nothing more efficient than grazing sheep for preventing the regrowth of woodland. Thus North Dean Wood was under threat from the charcoal burners who wished to chop it down and the woollen industry whose sheep would prevent any recovery. The miracle is that the woodland survived.

At one time the woodland would have filled the valley sides and the swampland in the valley bottom. Once draining techniques developed, communications could be driven through the valleys of the Calder and the Hebble and canal, road and rail links were all constructed here, and can be seen from several high vantage points during the walk.

Quarrying was also an important industry in and around the woods and more than 500 men were employed during the 19th century as the mill towns expanded and needed their new streets flagging with millstone grit. In these days of conservation it comes

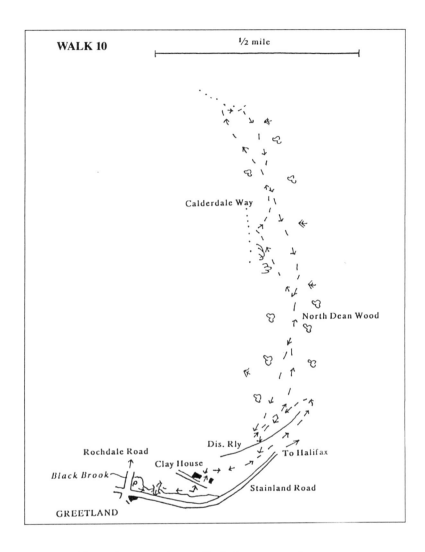

WALK 10

½ mile

Calderdale Way

North Dean Wood

Rochdale Road

Dis. Rly

Clay House

Black Brook

To Halifax

Stainland Road

GREETLAND

as something of a surprise to find that more than a century ago beech trees were actually planted to hide the great scars on the landscape gouged out by quarries. Some of these beeches are now approaching glorious maturity and their fallen leaves add colour to a winter walk and their triangular seeds provide good food for the common chaffinch and the occasional much rarer brambling which only occur in the winter. The botany of the area is interesting rather than spectacular but depending upon the season wood sorrel, dogs mercury, lesser celandine, golden saxifrage, wood anemone, bluebell and yellow archangel are all found here. Lily of the valley is one of the rare species found in North Dean and there is often a good crop of bilberry growing among the heather. We have gathered enough fruit here to make a couple of pies and a gallon of wine.

The study of trees has long been a hobby of ours and Dean Wood is of particular interest because both of the two species of oak found in Britain can be found here. The common or pedunculate oak *Querus robur* is actually more common in the south of England than in the north but a careful search around Dean Wood will reveal a few specimens among the dominant Sessile or Durmast oak *Quercus patrae*. The differences are as follows. The common oak grows mainly in the south east of England and the midlands where the soil is deep and loamy, whereas the Durmast is distributed to the north and west where the soil is more shallow and sandy. The latter is therefore more common in Dean Wood although we have found both and a few hybrids between the two. The acorns of the common oak are carried on a stalk. The scientific name for a stalk is a peduncle and this is why we have the name Pedunculate oak. There are also long green stripes on the fresh acorn. With the Durmast oak there is no stalk and no stripes. The leaves of the Durmast, however, have long stalks and a hairy under surface. Those of the common oak have much shorter stalks and are hairless. The buds of both species are carried in clusters at the end of a branch but those of the common oak are smaller and less pointed as those of the pedunculate oak.

Oak apples are often confused with acorns and labelled as fruits. Actually they are examples of galls and are caused by a tiny chalcid wasp. The females lay their eggs in the bud of the oak and the tree reacts by growing a cancer-like structure around the egg. The larva which emerges from the egg feeds on the gall and does not damage the rest of the tree. When ready to emerge as an adult the wasp burrows its way out of the oak apple and you can see the small exit hole through which it left.

During this very pretty walk there are many young oak trees which add colour especially during the winter. Whereas old oak trees tend to lose their leaves in autumn, young trees hold on to theirs which turn a lovely russet brown. They remain in position until pushed out by the new leaves which develop during the spring.

Because of its rich natural history North Dean is one area which should be regularly visited. Being so close to an industrial centre the beginning of the walk looks very uninviting. Within 400 yards, however, you are in wonderfully interesting countryside and enfolded by one of England's few remaining areas of wildwoods.

Around Dauber Bridge
and Hollin Hey

Access: From Halifax follow the A646 to Mytholmroyd. Turn left onto the B6138. There is only limited parking close to Dauber Bridge but if you feel really energetic you can walk from Mytholmroyd.

The Route:
CROSS the bridge, which is in a very rundown area, and find a footpath signed left and climbing narrow stone steps. At the top is a gate stile. Turn left. Cross three fields and then look for a stile in the corner. Turn right and pass between a stone wall on the right and a poultry farm on the left. Meet a road and turn right and then immediate left. Ignore Low Bank Farm and follow Stake Lane to Hollin Hey Wood. Much of this route is covered by old causey stones which can be slippy in wet or cold weather. After a steep climb up the causey turn right along a path signed Hollin Hey Bank. On the right is a stone wall whilst to the left is an ancient holly wood. When the paths divide follow the left fork up a steep slope and then swing right around a wall and close to a ruined barn. Bear left again up a grassy track between yet more tall holly trees. Do not pass through a field gate but bear right into a wood by passing through a stile. From a stone wall at the end of the wood pass a substantial outcrop of gritstone rocks on the right. There is a handy seat on the summit of the walk which is an ideal spot for a picnic. There is a farm up to the left. The path descends steeply into a dip above which are the so-called Robin Hood's Rocks. Pass a blue sign on the left labelled *"MCWW 15" Main"*. Beneath this is the line of the pipe from Withens Clough Reservoir to Morley. Keep descending and ignore any paths signed to the right. Cross a small stream and then pass through a stile and across a field. At the next wall turn right and follow a yellow sign. Keep a wall on the left and Holderness Wood is on the right. The descent is now very steep, and at the bottom turn left through a stile. Descend to cottages along a walled area. This is causeyed. This reaches Mid Birks Cottages dated 1612 and then past Twist Clough and Beech Cottages. At the road turn right. Pass Spa Cottages on the right. There is an alternative route here. The energetic can descend to the river and follow a footpath to Dauber Bridge. Equally interesting is the road route which follows the line of the 19th century turnpike road to Dauber Bridge and the starting point. Look out to the right for a well preserved milestone made for the Mytholmroyd and Blackstone Edge Road. It tells us we are

in the district of Erringden and that Rochdale is 11 miles away with Mytholmroyd 1¾ miles and Halifax 7¼ miles in the opposite direction. Pass Lower Clough Foot Restaurant on the left and Thornber Chicks "factory" on the right. Pass a recently renovated caravan park down to the left close to the stream which comes down from Crag Vale.

Our Walk:

WE all know holly as the tree which provides us with our Christmas decorations or as a hedgerow tree. To find woods dominated by holly is most unusual these days which is why this walk should be cherished by naturalists. Hollin means holly and Hey means wood so here we have a holly wood. The tree grows very, very slowly and there are so many large specimens in the wood that it must be of ancient origin.

The scientific name for the holly is Ilex Aquifolium, the latter being mentioned by the Roman historian Pliny and it means "needle-leaf". The Romans had a December festival which they called Saturnalia during which presents were wrapped up and garlanded with holly. Perhaps the Celts also had a similar mid-winter ceremony. The fact that the red berries could represent the blood of Christ ensured that the Christians took over the holly as a religious tree. Until Prince Albert married Queen Victoria and brought the spruce from Germany as the Christmas tree the holly was indeed the *Holy* tree of Christmas.

The female and male flowers are almost always carried on separate trees, and come into bloom in mid-May. The petals are waxy white and can be found by a careful look. The male flowers have four stamens and of course there are no female pistils. Female flowers have a four-lobed ovary surrounded by a four parted style and stigma. There are only rudimentary and obviously infertile anthers. Both sexes have scented flowers which attract insects such as flies and bees which pollinate them. The berries produced on the female trees are poisonous to humans, but birds can eat them and spread the seeds. These do not germiante the following spring but the first shoots appear in the second spring.

Holly was in great demand in the old days its ivory white wood being fine grained and much appreciated by carvers. It is, however, difficult to season as it soon warps and is therefore no good at all for outdoor work. It used to be dyed black and used as a substitute for the foreign and more expensive ebony in the production of teapot and whip handles and walking sticks. Holly is said to make wonderful fire wood. The berries and bark were once collected and mashed up to make sticky bird lime. This was smeared on branches and birds perching on these were trapped and eaten. These days we have supermarkets and butchers shops but long ago our ancestors had to catch and kill their own protein.

We have enjoyed many visits to Hollin Hey and have taken several friends who have all been fascinated by one of the most

42

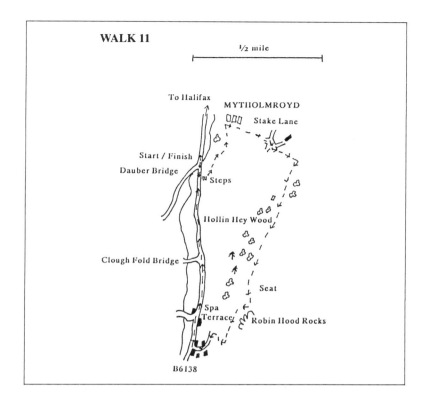

WALK 11

½ mile

To Halifax

MYTHOLMROYD

Stake Lane

Start / Finish
Dauber Bridge

Steps

Hollin Hey Wood

Clough Fold Bridge

Seat

Spa
Terrace   Robin Hood Rocks

B6138

impressive holly woods to be found in Britain.

Holly is an evergreen which means that the trees do not lose their leaves all at once but gradually over the year, but they do not produce good picnicking areas for very obvious and painful reasons. There are, however, several excellent areas for picnics, our favourite being around Robin Hood's Rocks. Many heathery dells here are lovely quiet sun traps. Robin Hood does seem to have been an impressive traveller and turns up in hundreds of places in Yorkshire and Lancashire all well to the north of Sherwood. There must have been many outlaws over the centuries and they have all become synonymous with Robin Hood. It is however, easy to imagine the Merrie Men finding refuge in the woodland area below Robin Hood's Rocks.

Holly woods are not ideal habitats for birds but mistle thrush, song thrush, blackbird and wood pigeon all nest among the prickles. The warm open areas are dominated by birch, oak and beech with an understorey made up of broom, heather and dog rose. This area is much richer in birds especially in late spring and early summer and on one June day we listened to the song of wood warbler, chiff chaff, redstart, tree pipit, whitethroat, blue tit, robin, wren but none could equal the lovely notes of the blackbird and song thrush.

Some of the walks described in this book pass so close to houses and farms that it is not fair to begin at dawn, but this is one which can be enjoyed early in the morning as the birds below Robin Hood's Rocks react to the rising sun by bursting into glorious song.

Hebden Bridge and Heptonstall

Access: From Halifax follow the A646 to Hebden Bridge. There are several car parks in the town but these can rapidly fill up. This is particularly so in the summer as Hebden Bridge is attracting more and more tourists. An answer may be park in Heptonstall and reverse the direction of the walk. Heptonstall is reached by following the A646 towards Todmorden. On the outskirts of the town there is a set of traffic lights. Heptonstall is to the right but there is no right turn. Proceed forward to a turning circle just beyond a garage. Use this and turn back towards Hebden Bridge and at the traffic lights bear left uphill. After a short distance turn left to Heptonstall where there is a large car park and a small but excellent fish and chip shop.

The Route:
FROM the old Hebden Bridge find the sign indicating Heptonstall. Climb steeply up the old packhorse route called the Buttress. Pass an old graveyard towards the top on the right. Meet a road. Turn right and then almost immediately left up stone steps with a hand rail on the left. At the junction of another road there is a welcome seat on the opposite side of the road. If you do not need a rest, turn right up the often busy road into Heptonstall. From this road there are splendid views down to the right across ancient birch woods growing on sloping ground. Many interesting buildings in the village can be seen by deviating either to the right or left from the main street on which stand two hotels serving bar snacks, the Cross and the White Lion. Continue to the top of the street which is cobbled and steep. At the end of the village look up to the right. Here is a stile leading to an old causeyed packhorse route back down into the village. This emerges close to the Wesleyan Chapel which is best explored at this point of the walk. From the village retrace your steps to the seat at the top of the stepped path. Descend the steps to the next road. Turn right. Just after the 30 mph sign do not proceed to the footpath signed left but turn very sharply to the left and follow a handrail down to the right around a house called Lee Mount. The path descends very steeply via houses on Moss Lane to Hebden Bridge.

Our Walk:
THIS is really a town walk taking in Hebden Bridge and Heptonstall but there is plenty to see and in winter we often take a whole day over it. In summer, however, we combine this with walk No. 8 along Hardcastle Crags which is close to both Heptonstall

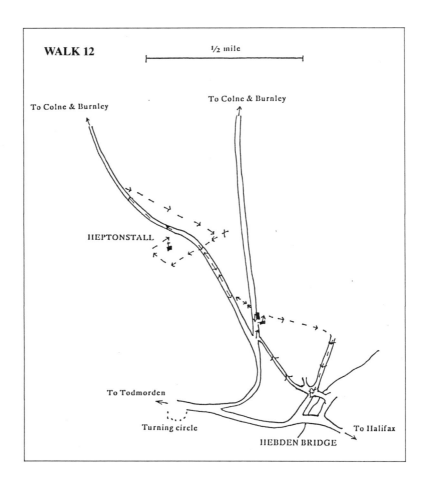

WALK 12

½ mile

To Colne & Burnley

To Colne & Burnley

HEPTONSTALL

To Todmorden

Turning circle

To Halifax

HEBDEN BRIDGE

and Hebden Bridge. We started our walk at Hebden Bridge itself which was built in 1510 to replace a wooden structure. In the days when the valley bottom was a swamp susceptible to regular flooding Heptonstall was constructed on the hillside overlooking the wet woodland. A packhorse track led down from Heptonstall to its bridge at Hebden. Once the valley was drained a settlement grew up around the bridge. As the Industrial Revolution gathered pace, Hebden Bridge became the focus of attention and Heptonstall was left as a handloom weaving village in a wonderful time warp.

We followed the old packhorse track which is still quite distinct up into Heptonstall and then we took our time walking around the old town which has much of interest on offer and is now protected by a conservation order.

46

The best place to start, providing it is open, is in the town museum from which the rest of the exploration can be planned. It is situated in the old Grammar School built in 1642. It is a pity that the local administrators cannot afford to open this splendid little place at times other than at weekends and on weekdays during the summer. The old schoolroom has been retained and there is also an exhibition of the infamous work of the 17th century coiners of Crag Vale, an evil bunch led by David Hartley and whose domain was seen from walk No. 9. The coiners worked by clipping bits of silver from coins and then melting down the metal to produce new coins. David Hartley was arrested in Halifax, hanged in York and eventually buried in Heptonstall churchyard. Actually Heptonstall has not one church but two, the ruin of an ancient church over-looking the more modern church across the graveyard which they both share.

Also in Heptonstall's main street are a number of three storeyed weavers' cottages and the old village pump just beyond the post office and the old Piece Hall where the pieces of wool made in the cottages were sold to the wholesalers. This is now a private dwelling. Signed from the main street but best approached along the causey from the top of the village is a Wesleyan Chapel built in 1764 and incorporating some design features suggested by John Wesley himself. The chapel is octagonal in shape and is still used for worship being the oldest such chapel still in use for worship. At one time the minister here was the grandfather of Rudyard Kipling who spent some of his youth in the area before making his reputation in India.

Although this walk is mainly urban there is a great deal of natural history to be seen without following walk No. 8 into the crags. It was just off the old packhorse track some years ago that we saw a hedgehog behaving in a most unusual manner. When we first saw it we thought it was dead and covered in a white mildew, but then we saw it move we realised that it was spitting saliva all over its spines. Other naturalists have observed this behaviour and it has been called "self annointing". Hedgehogs doing this look like an animated scrubbing brush covered in soapy suds. No firm reason has been given for the behaviour but a few guesses have been made. Some say that the hedgehog sucks at unpleasant material and spreads it over the spines of its body either to kill off the fleas and lice which often cover its body whilst others say the behaviour makes it unpalatable to predators. Whatever the reason it is behaviour unique to the hedgehog and very strange indeed. This event took place in June, but this must be good hedgehog country because on a stormy wet August morning we watched another spiny beast swim across a little stream running down from Heptonstall to the river Hebden.

A few years ago during a February snowstorm we saw a stoat in ermine cross the road below Heptonstall leading from Hebden Bridge to Burnley, the only part of its fur which was black was the tip of its tail and a spot on the nape of its neck. Most stoats in Scotland turn white for the winter and hardly any in southern England change, but in this area a few individuals change and at one time when fur was used extensively for clothing an ermine stoat pelt was very valuable.

This is true mammal country but the bird list is almost as impressive with peregrine, merlin, short and long eared, little and tawny owls all being recorded. Sparrowhawks breed close by and grey wagtails nest along the edges of the little streams.

The descent back down to Hebden Bridge provides stunning views and shows how the new town was built in layers above the valley bottom out of the way of the occasional flood when the waters which powered the early mills ran out of control.

It is fitting that the last walk in this book should provide such a balance between history, industrial archaeology and natural history. These three things are our reasons for walking as well as to provide a black labrador with exercise.